THE POWER OF YOUR ENVIRONMENT

HOW YOUR SURROUNDINGS SHAPE YOUR LIFE

By

Nick Imoru

Achievers Publishing
Calgary, Canada

THE POWER OF YOUR ENVIRONMENT: HOW YOUR SURROUNDINGS SHAPE YOUR LIFE
Copyright © 2024 By Nicholas Imoru

ISBN: 978-1-989291-11-5

Published in Canada, by
Achievers Publishing

Canadian Cataloguing in Publication (CIP)
A Record of this Publication is available from the Library and Archives Canada (LAC).

"The right of Nicholas Imoru to be identified as the author of this work has been asserted in accordance with the Copyright, Designs and Patents Act 1988 sections 77 and 78"

All rights reserved. Written permission must be secured from the publisher to use or reproduce any part of the book except for brief quotations in critical reviews, magazines or articles.

For further information or permission, address:
Achievers Publishing
Calgary, Canada
E-mail: info@achieverspublishing.com
www.achieverspublishing.com

Printed in Canada for Achievers Publishing

THE POWER OF YOUR ENVIRONMENT

HOW YOUR SURROUNDINGS SHAPE YOUR LIFE

Dedication

This book is dedicated to Living Faith Church Worldwide (Winners Chapel International) and Scripture Union (SU) — two transformative environments that have profoundly shaped my life.

Scripture Union laid the foundation in the early stages of my life, nurturing my faith and instilling in me the principles that would guide my journey. Without its influence, I would not be the person I am today.

Winners Chapel International has been a life-giving environment, providing the fertile soil for my faith, purpose, and vision to flourish through its teachings, community, and unwavering commitment to the Word of God.

Thank you for being places of inspiration, growth, and spiritual empowerment. May this book reflect the influence of these remarkable environments and inspire others to cultivate spaces that lead to growth and greatness.

Table of Contents

Contents

INTRODUCTION: OVERVIEW OF THE CONCEPT

How Environments Influence Behaviors, Thoughts, and Feelings

From the moment we wake up, our environment begins to affect how we feel, think, and act. Whether we are aware of it or not, our surroundings play a profound role in shaping our identity and our experiences in life. The books we read, the shows we watch, the music we listen to, and the people we interact with all form part of a complex and dynamic environment that influences us in ways we may not even notice. This influence extends beyond mere external factors; it seeps into our thoughts, beliefs, and ultimately the decisions we make.

Consider the common scenario of stepping into a room that is cluttered and chaotic. You might not realize it, but the disarray around you often leads to feelings of anxiety, distraction, and lowered productivity. On the other hand, when you enter a clean, well-organized space, you may find yourself feeling calmer, more focused, and energized. This is just one example of how our physical environment affects our internal state.

However, environment is not limited to physical spaces alone. Social environments—composed of the people we surround ourselves with—are just as crucial. The attitudes, behaviors, and energy of the people in our lives influence us deeply, shaping our mindsets and, by extension, the trajectory of our lives. As it says in Proverbs 13:20 (KJV), *"He that walketh with wise men shall be wise: but a companion of fools shall be destroyed."* This verse reveals a fundamental truth: the people you associate with can elevate you or bring you down, depending on their influence. Similarly, our mental environment—what we feed our minds through media, conversations, and even our self-talk—affects our worldview and our daily choices.

Importance of Becoming Aware of the Impact of One's Environment

Becoming conscious of your environment is the first critical step toward understanding its powerful influence on your life. Many people go through life without ever considering how their surroundings are shaping them. They may feel stuck, unmotivated, or overwhelmed, never realizing that their environment could be the primary culprit behind their struggles.

The Bible speaks frequently about the power of environment, especially in relation to our spiritual walk. In Psalm 1:1-3 (NIV), the psalmist writes, *"Blessed is the one who does not walk in step with the wicked or stand in the way that sinners take or sit in the company of mockers, but whose delight is in the law of the Lord, and who meditates on his law day and night. That person is like a tree planted by streams of water, which yields its fruit in season and whose leaf does not wither— whatever they do prospers."* The psalmist reveals that avoiding negative influences and immersing oneself in godly surroundings leads to fruitfulness and prosperity. In the same way, recognizing and evaluating the impact of your environment will allow you to make necessary changes that align your life with your true potential.

Take a moment to reflect: What kinds of environments are you placing yourself in? Is your physical space conducive to peace, productivity, and focus? Are the people in your life encouraging you to grow, or are they holding you back with negativity and doubt? Are you feeding your mind with thoughts and materials that elevate your spirit, or are you consuming content that weighs you down?

Understanding the direct correlation between environment and outcome is crucial for personal development. We must constantly assess our surroundings and make deliberate choices to foster an environment that nurtures our growth.

Purpose of the Book:

The goal of this book is clear: to help you recognize the profound impact your environment has on your life and to empower you to make conscious, strategic decisions to reshape your surroundings for positive growth and success. Whether it's altering your physical space, changing your social circle, or realigning your mindset, you hold the power to create an environment that supports your goals.

Throughout the book, we will delve into how environments affect various aspects of your life—your physical health, mental well-being, productivity, relationships, and spiritual walk with God. We will explore practical steps for making changes in each area, grounded in real-world examples and biblical principles.

As you embark on this journey, remember the words of Romans 12:2 (NIV): *"Do not conform to the pattern of this world, but be transformed by the renewing of your mind. Then you will be able to test and approve what God's will is—his good, pleasing and perfect will."* Transforming your environment is not just about rearranging furniture or avoiding certain people; it's about renewing your mind and creating conditions that align with God's will for your life. When your environment reflects the person you aspire to be, growth becomes natural and inevitable.

In the following chapters, you will learn how to evaluate your current environment and make the necessary changes to optimize it for success. This book serves as both a guide and a challenge—a guide to understanding the powerful role of your environment and a challenge to take control of it for your own benefit. Are you ready to make those changes? The journey starts now.

CHAPTER 1: UNDERSTANDING YOUR ENVIRONMENT

1.1 Definition of Environment

When we talk about the environment, many people instantly think of their physical surroundings: the places they live, work, and spend time. While this is certainly a part of it, the concept of the environment extends much further. The environment encompasses everything that surrounds us, both visible and invisible, tangible and intangible.

Let's begin by breaking it down into three broad categories:

- **Physical Space:** This includes your home, workplace, car, and any other physical spaces where you spend your time. It's the space you physically occupy, and it holds a significant influence over your well-being. A cluttered, disorganized home can lead to feelings of stress and overwhelm, while a clean, well-arranged space promotes peace and productivity.

- **Social Circles:** The people you spend time with—family, friends, colleagues, and even acquaintances—are a key part of your environment. Proverbs 27:17 (NIV) tells us, *"As iron sharpens iron, so one person sharpens another."* The people around you can either sharpen you, encouraging growth and positivity, or dull your edge, pulling you into negative habits and thinking.

- **Media Consumption:** In today's digital age, the media you consume—whether it be books, music, television, social media, or podcasts—is a vital part of your environment. What you fill your mind with on a daily basis influences your thoughts, behaviors, and even your worldview. Philippians 4:8 (NIV) reminds us, *"Finally, brothers and sisters, whatever is true, whatever is noble, whatever is right, whatever is pure, whatever is lovely, whatever is admirable—if* *anything is excellent or praiseworthy—think about such things."* This verse encourages us to be mindful of what we allow into our minds, as it plays a significant role in shaping who we are.

Your environment is a combination of all these elements. It is the combination of everything you expose yourself to physically, socially, and mentally. Recognizing these components allow us to begin to evaluate their influence over our lives.

1.2 Influence on Behavior

Our surroundings shape how we think, how we feel, and ultimately how we act. This influence begins from the moment we are born and continues throughout our lives. Although we often underestimate the power of our environment, it is constantly affecting us in ways we may not consciously recognize.

1. **How Environment Shapes Thoughts**: The thoughts that fill your mind daily are directly tied to what you see, hear, and experience in your environment. For instance, if you are surrounded by pessimistic or negative people, your thoughts

will likely reflect that negativity. You may find yourself thinking that life is unfair, or that opportunities are limited, because those around you constantly communicate such ideas. Conversely, if you are surrounded by people who think positively and encourage one another, your thoughts will align with that energy, making you more likely to see challenges as opportunities and to maintain hope in difficult situations.

A good example of how environment affects thoughts is found in the story of the 12 spies sent by Moses to scout the Promised Land in Numbers 13. Ten of the spies were surrounded by fear, reporting that they couldn't conquer the land because the inhabitants were giants. Their negative environment caused them to focus on their limitations. On the other hand, Joshua and Caleb, who were surrounded by faith in God's promises, believed they could conquer the land. The same physical environment (the Promised Land) created two different perspectives because of the differing mental environments of the spies.

2. **How Environment Affects Feelings**: The emotional atmosphere in your environment greatly affects how you feel. If you are in a space filled with stress and chaos—whether that is a cluttered home or a workplace full of tension—your emotional state will reflect that. You may feel overwhelmed, anxious, or unmotivated. On the other hand, a peaceful environment, free of clutter and negativity, can contribute to feelings of calm, focus, and happiness.

   In Proverbs 15:13 (NIV), it says, *"A happy heart makes the face cheerful, but heartache crushes the spirit."* Your surroundings can play a crucial role in shaping your emotional well-being. Positive environments breed joy and contentment, while negative environments foster feelings of sadness, frustration, or fear.

3. **How Environment Dictates Actions**: Ultimately, your actions are the product of your thoughts and feelings. When you find yourself in

an environment conducive to growth, you naturally begin to take actions that align with personal development, health, and success. If your surroundings encourage discipline, organization, and positivity, your actions will reflect these qualities. However, if you are in an environment where laziness, disorder, or negativity reign, your actions are likely to follow suit.

This concept is beautifully illustrated in Psalm 1:1-3 (NIV), which states: *"Blessed is the one who does not walk in step with the wicked or stand in the way that sinners take or sit in the company of mockers, but whose delight is in the law of the Lord... That person is like a tree planted by streams of water, which yields its fruit in season and whose leaf does not wither—whatever they do prospers."* The psalmist makes it clear that actions and behaviors are heavily influenced by who we associate with and the environments we immerse ourselves in. A person who surrounds themselves with righteousness and godly influences will naturally prosper, just as a tree prospers when it is planted by life-giving water.

1.3 Invisible Forces at Play

Often, the most significant influences in our environment are the ones we don't immediately notice. These are the *invisible forces* that subtly shape our lives without our full awareness. Here are a few examples:

1. **Cultural Norms**: Every culture has its own set of values, expectations, and beliefs that are woven into the fabric of daily life. These cultural norms influence us profoundly, often dictating what we consider acceptable or unacceptable without us even realizing it. For instance, certain cultures prioritize hard work and achievement, while others may place greater emphasis on relaxation or family time. These invisible cultural expectations can shape how we view success, relationships, and even our sense of self-worth.

2. **Background Noise**: Sometimes, the background noise in our environment—whether

it's the news, social media, or the conversations of others—can subtly influence our thoughts, feelings, and actions. Even though we may not be paying attention to it, this noise is still shaping our perceptions and behavior. For instance, hearing constant negative news or being surrounded by gossip can lead to a more negative outlook on life, even if we aren't actively engaging with that content.

3. **Spiritual Atmospheres**: As believers, we know that the spiritual realm has a significant impact on our lives. The Bible teaches us that we are not just physical beings, but spiritual ones as well. Therefore, the spiritual atmosphere of the environments we enter is of great importance. Ephesians 6:12 (NIV) reminds us, *"For our struggle is not against flesh and blood, but against the rulers, against the authorities, against the powers of this dark world and against the spiritual forces of evil in the heavenly realms."* Spiritual environments—whether positive or negative—can shape our mood, attitude, and even our sense of spiritual well-being.

Surrounding ourselves with godly, faith-filled atmosphere is critical to maintaining spiritual strength.

4. **Unconscious Associations**: Our environment can create unconscious associations that influence how we respond to certain stimuli. For example, if you always relax on your couch after work, your mind may begin to associate that space with rest and relaxation, making it difficult to do productive tasks while sitting there. These subtle associations can dictate how we feel and act in different spaces, often without us realizing it.

In conclusion, while the environment may seem external and passive, it actively shapes who we are on every level. Understanding its role in our lives is the first step in mastering our surroundings and using them to our advantage. As we continue to explore this concept, remember the words of Proverbs 4:23 (NIV): *"Above all else, guard your heart, for everything you do flows from it."* Your environment is a direct influence on your heart—guard it carefully by creating surroundings that nurture growth, peace, and positivity.

CHAPTER 2: THE PHYSICAL ENVIRONMENT

2.1 The Impact of Physical Space

Your physical environment—the spaces where you live, work, and spend time—affects not only your mood but also your productivity, mental clarity, and overall well-being. Every object in your home or office either contributes to or detracts from the atmosphere of peace, order, and focus. The state of your physical surroundings reflects, in many ways, the state of your mind.

An organized and intentional living space offers more than just a tidy appearance; it is a tool for personal and professional growth. In Proverbs 24:3-4 (NIV), we read, *"By wisdom a house is built, and through understanding it is established; through knowledge its rooms are filled with rare and beautiful treasures."* This verse emphasizes the need for thoughtful and intentional design in our homes. Just as a house requires wisdom in its construction, so too does a living or working space require careful organization and attention to detail.

When your physical environment is cluttered and chaotic, it creates a mental burden that may not be immediately obvious. Clutter competes for your attention, pulling you away from the tasks at hand, making it difficult to focus. Whether it's a messy kitchen counter, a cluttered desk, or an overcrowded closet, physical disorder can quickly lead to feelings of overwhelm. On the other hand, an organized space—where everything has its place and there is room to breathe—can foster a sense of peace and control. It creates a foundation for productivity and success.

Your home or workspace should be designed with intention. Think about the spaces where you spend the most time: Are they optimized for what you need to do? Is your home a sanctuary where you can relax and recharge, or does it feel chaotic and stressful? Is your office a place where you can focus and get work done, or are distractions pulling you away from your goals?

The Bible highlights the importance of intentional environments in many places. Consider Jesus' words in Matthew 6:6 (NIV), *"But when you pray, go into your room, close the door and pray to your Father, who is unseen. Then your Father, who sees what is done in secret, will reward you."* Jesus instructs us to seek a quiet, private place to connect with God, emphasizing the need for intentional physical spaces that allow for focus and spiritual growth. In the same way, your home and workspace should be places that foster growth, whether that's personal, professional, or spiritual.

2.2 How Adjustments Can Boost Productivity

The power of transforming your physical environment lies in making thoughtful adjustments that align with your goals. Small changes—like decluttering a room or rearranging a workspace—can have an outsized impact on your productivity, mental clarity, and emotional well-being.

One of the simplest yet most powerful ways to improve your space is through decluttering. Clutter not only makes it hard to find things when you need them, but it also creates mental noise. When there is too much "stuff" in your physical environment, your brain has more stimuli to process, making it harder to focus. Decluttering is not just about throwing things away, but about creating a space that reflects your values and priorities. When you remove the unnecessary, you make room for what truly matters.

Decluttering can have both a symbolic and practical effect. For example, many people find that clearing their home office of old paperwork, unnecessary gadgets, or irrelevant decor leads to a clearer mind and sharper focus. It creates a more inviting space to work, which translates into higher productivity and efficiency.

Another key element is creating focused workspaces. In today's world of remote work and digital distractions, it's easy to blur the lines between work and relaxation. Many people try to work from their living room couches or even their beds, but these areas are not designed for productivity. The problem is that our minds form associations between spaces and activities. If you often relax on your couch or sleep in your bed, your mind may resist doing focused work in those same spaces.

Creating a dedicated workspace—whether it's a separate office or simply a corner of a room with a desk—helps signal to your brain that this is a place for work. A stand-up desk, for example, can encourage better posture, increase energy, and improve focus. Similarly, adding elements like a comfortable chair, good lighting, and tools for organization can make all the difference in staying productive throughout the day.

The Bible speaks to the importance of order and diligence in all areas of life. Ecclesiastes 9:10 (NIV) reminds us, *"Whatever your hand finds to do, do it with all your might."* This scripture encourages us to take action with full dedication and energy. A well-organized workspace allows us to do exactly that—to commit ourselves fully to the tasks before us, unhindered by distractions or disarray.

2.3 Case Studies:

The impact of physical space on our lives is well illustrated by real-world examples. There is a story of a real estate couple whose relationship was deeply affected by their cluttered bedroom. The husband and wife had allowed their bedroom to become a secondary office space, filled with paperwork and clutter. This not only created an eyesore but also introduced stress and anxiety into what should have been a restful, intimate environment.

When asked about their relationship, the wife admitted to feeling frustrated and disconnected. She described how her husband would spend late nights working at the desk in their bedroom, surrounded by piles of paperwork, while she tried to sleep. The clutter became a constant reminder of their financial concerns and work stress, creating a wedge between them. Their physical environment was negatively influencing both their emotions and their relationship.

Once they recognized this, they made the conscious decision to separate their workspace from their bedroom. By removing the clutter and designating the bedroom as a place for rest and connection, they noticed an immediate improvement in their relationship. The physical change led to emotional healing. Their story exemplifies the profound effect that physical space can have on the dynamics of personal relationships.

Another powerful example comes from the story of using a stand-up desk in a home office. One individual noticed that sitting all day was draining his energy and causing him to be less productive. After switching to a stand-up desk, he experienced higher energy levels, improved posture, and greater focus throughout the day. This small adjustment to his physical environment made a significant difference in how he felt and performed during his workday.

These stories remind us that the spaces we occupy are not neutral. They either serve us or hinder us, depending on how we use them. The key is to make our physical environment work for us, supporting our goals and fostering our well-being. As we are reminded in 1 Corinthians 14:40 (NIV), *"But everything should be done in a fitting and orderly way."* This applies not only to how we live our lives but also to how we organize the spaces in which we live and work.

By consciously organizing and optimizing our physical environment, we can create spaces that uplift us, enhance our productivity, and contribute to our emotional and relational well-being. The power of a well-organized space cannot be overstated—it is a foundational aspect of building a life of peace, focus, and success.

CHAPTER 3: THE SOCIAL ENVIRONMENT

3.1 The People Around You

The social environment you surround yourself with plays an immense role in shaping your mindset, attitudes, and ultimately, your life choices. Human beings are inherently social creatures; we are constantly influenced by the people around us, whether we realize it or not. Our friends, family, colleagues, and acquaintances all contribute to the mental and emotional atmosphere in which we live.

The Bible provides profound wisdom on this matter. Proverbs 13:20 (NIV) states, *"Walk with the wise and become wise, for a companion of fools suffers harm."* This passage highlights a fundamental truth: the people you associate with will either elevate you or bring you down. Their attitudes and behaviors will inevitably rub off on you. If you surround yourself with wise, positive, and motivated people, your mindset will reflect those qualities. Conversely, if you spend time with individuals who are negative, lazy, or critical, you will find yourself adopting those attitudes.

Take a moment to think about the people in your immediate circle. How do their attitudes influence you? Do they encourage you to strive for excellence, or do they pull you down with complaints, gossip, or pessimism? Your social circle can either be a source of strength or a stumbling block on your journey toward personal growth and success.

Research and common experience reveal that we tend to conform to the behaviors of those we spend the most time with. This conformity can be subtle—adopting the habits, speech patterns, or attitudes of those around us—or it can be more direct, as we are influenced by their opinions and actions. 1 Corinthians 15:33 (NIV) warns, *"Do not be misled: 'Bad company corrupts good character.'"* This verse speaks to the reality that even if you have good intentions and strong values, the wrong company can lead you astray.

It's essential to carefully evaluate your social environment and assess how it is impacting your mindset. Ask yourself: Are the people around me pushing me toward growth, or are they holding me back? Do they encourage me to live according to my highest values, or do they lead me into negative habits? Recognizing the influence of your social circle is the first step toward building a more supportive and growth-oriented environment.

3.2 Social Distancing for Growth

Growth often requires change, and sometimes that change involves creating distance between yourself and negative influences. The term "social distancing" gained prominence during the pandemic, but in the context of personal development, it refers to the process of distancing yourself from people who are toxic, draining, or unsupportive of your goals. This is not an easy decision, especially when it involves people you have known for a long time or those you care about deeply. However, it is often necessary for your personal and spiritual growth.

Consider what Hebrews 12:1 (NIV) says: *"Therefore, since we are surrounded by such a great cloud of witnesses, let us throw off everything that hinders and the sin that so easily entangles. And let us run with perseverance the race marked out for us."* The phrase "everything that hinders" can apply to people who are a negative influence in your life. To move forward, you must release anything or anyone that weighs you down, preventing you from reaching your full potential.

When you distance yourself from negative influences, you make room for positive, uplifting relationships that encourage your growth. Surrounding yourself with positive people creates an environment of accountability, motivation, and mutual support. These relationships are vital for your success, as they provide the emotional and mental energy needed to stay focused on your goals.

In the book of Proverbs, we are reminded of the value of positive, growth-oriented relationships. Proverbs 27:17 (NIV) tells us, *"As iron sharpens iron, so one person sharpens another."* Positive people help you become better—they challenge you, inspire you, and hold you accountable for your actions. They are the ones who celebrate your successes and offer constructive feedback during setbacks.

Distancing yourself from negative influences doesn't mean cutting people off in a harsh or judgmental way. Instead, it's about protecting your mental and emotional health. It's about creating boundaries that allow you to prioritize your growth and well-being. For example, you might limit your interactions with individuals who are constantly negative or critical, or you may choose to engage with them in settings where their influence is less potent. By doing so, you can create a social environment that supports your aspirations and dreams.

Jesus Himself modeled this concept in His ministry. While He spent time with sinners and those in need, He also withdrew to places of solitude to pray and refocus (Luke 5:16). This practice of distancing—even temporarily—allowed Him to recharge and maintain His focus on His mission. Likewise, you must find time to separate yourself from influences that pull you away from your purpose, making room for relationships that encourage growth.

3.3 Broken People and Relationships

One of the most common traps in relationships is seeking healing or fulfillment from people who are themselves broken or struggling. While it may seem logical to find comfort in others who share your pain, the truth is that two broken people cannot fully heal each other. Instead, they often end up reinforcing each other's wounds, perpetuating cycles of hurt and dysfunction.

The Bible offers wisdom on this matter. In Matthew 15:14 (NIV), Jesus says, *"If the blind lead the blind, both will fall into a pit."* This verse vividly illustrates the dangers of looking to others who are equally lost or hurt to guide you. While you may share a common experience of pain, that alone is not enough to bring healing. Instead, both individuals may become trapped in their wounds, unable to rise above the challenges they face.

Broken relationships can often lead to disappointment and unmet expectations. When you place your hope in someone who is also struggling, you may expect them to provide the comfort, support, or guidance you need.

However, because they are dealing with their own issues, they are often unable to meet those expectations. This creates a cycle of frustration and pain, as both parties feel let down by the other.

In some cases, broken people may even enable each other's destructive behaviors. For example, if you are trying to overcome a bad habit, such as smoking or drinking, spending time with someone who shares that same habit can make it harder to break free. You may find yourselves reinforcing each other's unhealthy behaviors rather than supporting one another in the process of healing.

The Bible teaches that true healing comes from God, not from other people. Psalm 147:3 (NIV) says, *"He heals the brokenhearted and binds up their wounds."* While supportive relationships are important, they should never take the place of seeking healing and wholeness from God. It is only through Him that we find the strength and grace to heal our wounds and become whole.

If you are in a relationship where both parties are struggling, it's essential to recognize the limitations of what you can offer each other. Healing must first come from within—through your relationship with God, personal growth, and self-reflection. Only then can you be in a position to support someone else's healing journey.

It's also important to seek relationships with people who have already walked the path of healing and can offer you guidance, wisdom, and encouragement. These individuals can serve as mentors, helping you avoid the pitfalls of seeking healing from those who are still hurting. As Galatians 6:1-2 (NIV) advises, *"Brothers and sisters, if someone is caught in a sin, you who live by the Spirit should restore that person gently. But watch yourselves, or you also may be tempted. Carry each other's burdens, and in this way you will fulfill the law of Christ."* Surrounding yourself with spiritually mature people who have experienced healing allows you to receive the support you need to overcome your own struggles.

In conclusion, the social environment is one of the most critical aspects of your life. The people you allow into your circle will shape your mindset, influence your behaviors, and either support or hinder your growth. By distancing yourself from negative influences and choosing relationships that foster positivity and healing, you create an environment that empowers you to reach your full potential. Remember, true healing comes from God, and the relationships in your life should reflect that truth.

CHAPTER 4: ENVIRONMENTAL DESIGN FOR SUCCESS

4.1 Optimizing Your Environment for Growth

Success is not solely the result of willpower or discipline. Rather, much of our success in life comes from intentionally designing environments that foster growth, productivity, and positive behaviors. The Bible gives us many examples of the importance of setting the right conditions for growth, not only spiritually but also in all areas of life.

In the parable of the Sower (Matthew 13:3-9), Jesus explains how seeds sown in different environments—on rocky ground, among thorns, or on fertile soil—yield different results. The seeds that fall on fertile ground grow and bear fruit, while those on rocky or thorny ground struggle and eventually die. In the same way, our personal and professional goals can only flourish if they are nurtured in an environment designed to support them.

To optimize your environment for growth, the first step is to define your goals clearly. Once you know what you want to achieve—whether it's improving your health, advancing in your career, or deepening your spiritual life—you can begin to shape your surroundings in ways that make success more attainable.

Consider your physical space. Is it set up to help you stay focused and productive? A cluttered workspace can be distracting, while a clean, organized space can provide clarity and a sense of control. If your goal is to improve your fitness, is your environment supporting that? For instance, placing your workout gear in an easily accessible location can remove the friction that often prevents us from exercising. Similarly, setting up a specific area for prayer or meditation can strengthen your spiritual discipline by creating a space that encourages focus and connection with God.

As 1 Corinthians 14:40 (NIV) instructs, *"But everything should be done in a fitting and orderly way."* This principle can be applied to all aspects of your environment—whether it's how you arrange your workspace, your home, or even the digital environment you interact with daily. Order and intentionality create conditions where growth becomes natural rather than forced.

Beyond the physical, your social environment also plays a crucial role. Surround yourself with people who share your vision or who inspire you to grow. Proverbs 27:17 (NIV) tells us, *"As iron sharpens iron, so one person sharpens another."* When you align your social environment with your goals, you create an atmosphere of accountability and encouragement. Whether it's in the form of mentors, peers, or friends, these relationships are essential for keeping you on track.

4.2 Reducing Reliance on Willpower

One of the greatest misconceptions about success is that it requires a constant exertion of willpower. While willpower is an important tool, it is finite and easily depleted, especially when we are tired, stressed, or overwhelmed. Fortunately, by designing your environment strategically, you can reduce your reliance on willpower and make success easier to achieve.

James Clear, in his book *Atomic Habits*, explains that "environment is the invisible hand that shapes human behavior." By removing temptations and creating a space that aligns with your goals, you make it easier to make the right choices, even when your willpower is low.

Let's consider food as an example. If your goal is to eat healthier, but your kitchen is stocked with junk food, you will constantly have to fight the temptation to indulge in unhealthy snacks. However, if you remove the junk food and replace it with nutritious options, you won't need to rely on willpower to make healthy choices. You'll simply be following the path of least resistance—eating what's available.

This principle can be applied to any area of life. If your goal is to read more, keep books within easy reach—on your nightstand, in your living room, or on your desk. If you want to reduce distractions while working, eliminate or hide unnecessary apps from your phone or computer. Proverbs 4:27 (NIV) gives us practical advice in this regard: *"Do not turn to the right or the left; keep your foot from evil."* In other words, stay focused and remove distractions that may cause you to stray from your purpose.

The Bible also speaks about the importance of avoiding temptation. In Matthew 26:41 (NIV), Jesus says, *"Watch and pray so that you will not fall into temptation. The spirit is willing, but the flesh is weak."* Jesus acknowledges that even with the best intentions, we are prone to give in to our desires if we are not vigilant. By designing our environment to minimize temptation, we set ourselves up for success.

In addition to reducing temptations, environmental design can help automate positive habits. For example, if your goal is to spend more time in prayer or Bible study, you might create a morning routine that begins with sitting in a designated space where your Bible is already open and ready. The easier it is to engage in the habit, the more likely you are to follow through.

4.3 The Path of Least Resistance

Success often follows the path of least resistance. By structuring your environment in such a way that positive behaviors become the easiest option, you make growth almost inevitable. This is a powerful concept, as it removes much of the friction that comes from trying to force change through sheer effort.

In Genesis 1:31 (NIV), after God had finished His creation, it says, *"God saw all that he had made, and it was very good."* God created an environment where everything had its place, and it was designed to function perfectly in harmony. Likewise, we can design our personal environments to function smoothly, creating conditions where positive behaviors are the natural outcome.

Think of a river. Water flows where the resistance is lowest. If you want the water to flow in a particular direction, you don't force it; you simply remove the obstacles in its way. In the same way, if you want to encourage good habits, you need to remove the barriers that make those habits difficult and create a clear path toward success.

For example, if you want to increase your productivity at work, removing distractions such as unnecessary apps, clutter, or notifications will create a smoother flow of work. If your goal is to work out regularly, placing your exercise equipment in a convenient, visible spot will make it easier to get started. The more friction you remove, the more natural the behavior becomes.

In Romans 13:14 (NIV), Paul writes, *"Rather, clothe yourselves with the Lord Jesus Christ, and do not think about how to gratify the desires of the flesh."* Here, Paul encourages us to avoid even thinking about temptations, which is only possible when we create an environment that eliminates those desires. By structuring your environment to make positive behaviors the default, you remove the need to constantly battle your flesh.

The key to designing an environment for success lies in making the right behaviors as easy and automatic as possible, while making negative behaviors more difficult. When you structure your environment this way, success becomes less about willpower and more about creating the right conditions for growth. Over time, these small changes add up, leading to big results.

In conclusion, environmental design is a powerful tool for personal growth and success. By optimizing your environment to align with your goals, reducing your reliance on willpower, and creating a path of least resistance, you can make positive behaviors the default and achieve your objectives with greater ease. Just as God created the world in perfect order, we, too, can create environments that promote harmony and growth in our lives.

CHAPTER 5: ENVIRONMENT AND SPIRITUAL GROWTH

5.1 Godly Community and Personal Time with God

Spiritual growth, much like physical or mental growth, is deeply influenced by the environment in which it takes place. To grow spiritually, we need to immerse ourselves in environments that foster closeness to God, encourage faith, and provide opportunities for reflection and communion with the Lord. One of the most essential elements of spiritual growth is being part of a godly community—a community of believers who share a common faith and walk alongside us on our journey with God.

Hebrews 10:24-25 (NIV) says, *"And let us consider how we may spur one another on toward love and good deeds, not giving up meeting together, as some are in the habit of doing, but encouraging one another—and all the more as you see the Day approaching."* This verse highlights the importance of regular fellowship with other believers. A godly community provides accountability, encouragement, and support as we navigate the challenges of life and grow in our faith. Surrounding ourselves with people who are committed to spiritual growth helps us stay focused on our own walk with God, even during difficult times.

Godly communities also play a vital role in helping us stay grounded in truth. In a world filled with distractions and conflicting messages, being in fellowship with believers who uphold the teachings of the Bible helps us stay aligned with God's will. Proverbs 27:17 (NIV) reminds us, *"As iron sharpens iron, so one person sharpens another."* In the same way, believers sharpen each other through shared worship, Bible study, prayer, and mutual encouragement.

In addition to community, personal time with God is crucial for spiritual growth. While it is important to gather with others in worship and fellowship, personal time in prayer and meditation allows us to connect intimately with the Lord. Jesus Himself often withdrew to quiet places to pray and spend time alone with the Father. Luke 5:16 (NIV) tells us, *"But Jesus often withdrew to lonely places and prayed."* Jesus understood the value of setting aside time to commune with God away from the distractions and demands of life. Creating a quiet, sacred space for personal devotion fosters spiritual growth by allowing us to hear God's voice, reflect on His word, and be strengthened by His presence.

It is vital to cultivate both a godly community and a personal relationship with God, as both serve as essential elements of an environment that nurtures spiritual growth.

5.2 Influence on Spiritual Walk

While being in a godly environment promotes spiritual growth, being in the wrong environment can hinder or even stunt that growth. The Bible speaks clearly about the dangers of surrounding ourselves with influences that lead us away from God. When we allow ourselves to remain in environments filled with negativity, sin, or distractions, our spiritual progress can come to a standstill.

Psalm 1:1-2 (NIV) provides a clear warning about the influence of ungodly environments: *"Blessed is the one who does not walk in step with the wicked or stand in the way that sinners take or sit in the company of mockers, but whose delight is in the law of the Lord, and who meditates on his law day and night."* The psalmist paints a vivid picture of how the company we keep and the environment we choose to dwell in can either lead us closer to God or pull us away. Walking in the counsel of the wicked or standing in the way of sinners leads to spiritual stagnation, but meditating on the Word of God leads to growth and blessing.

Environments of constant negativity, gossip, or worldly distractions can cause our hearts to harden and our sensitivity to God's voice to dull. The more time we spend in environments that are disconnected from God's truth, the more we become desensitized to His presence. 1 Corinthians 15:33 (NIV) warns, *"Do not be misled: 'Bad company corrupts good character.'"* Even if we have strong faith, prolonged exposure to ungodly environments can slowly wear down our spiritual defenses, leading us to compromise or lose sight of our calling.

One common example is the workplace. Many people find themselves in jobs where the culture is highly competitive, materialistic, or unethical. While we may not always have control over our work environment, it's important to be intentional about how much influence we allow these negative environments to have over us. Setting boundaries—both emotional and spiritual—helps protect our spiritual walk. This may mean finding times throughout the day to pray, meditate on Scripture, or listen to worship music, even in challenging environments.

In some cases, God may call us to leave environments that are detrimental to our spiritual health altogether. Just as He called Abraham to leave his country, his people, and his father's household to follow Him (Genesis 12:1), there may be times when we need to make a radical change to preserve our spiritual growth. Trusting in God's guidance, even when it requires leaving behind what is familiar, can lead to greater spiritual rewards and a closer walk with Him.

5.3 Sowing into the Spirit vs. the Flesh

The Bible frequently draws a clear distinction between living by the Spirit and living by the flesh. The environments we choose to dwell in play a significant role in determining whether we are sowing into the Spirit or into the flesh. Galatians 6:7-8 (NIV) offers this wisdom: *"Do not be deceived: God cannot be mocked. A man reaps what he sows. Whoever sows to please their flesh, from the flesh will reap destruction; whoever sows to please the Spirit, from the Spirit will reap eternal life."*

The environment we immerse ourselves in often determines whether we are sowing into the Spirit or the flesh. For example, if we consistently expose ourselves to media, conversations, or activities that gratify the flesh—such as greed, lust, anger, or selfishness—we are sowing into the flesh. These environments may seem harmless at first, but over time, they lead to spiritual decay, as they feed desires and behaviors that pull us away from God.

In contrast, environments that encourage us to focus on God and His righteousness help us to sow into the Spirit. This includes surrounding ourselves with godly influences, spending time in worship and prayer, and meditating on Scripture. Romans 8:5-6 (NIV) highlights the importance of this distinction: *"Those who live according to the flesh have their minds set on what the flesh desires; but those who live in accordance with the Spirit have their minds set on what the Spirit desires. The mind governed by the flesh is death, but the mind governed by the Spirit is life and peace."*

Sowing into the Spirit leads to life and peace, while sowing into the flesh leads to destruction. This is why it is so crucial to carefully choose the environments we spend time in. Each environment has the potential to either bring us closer to God and to spiritual fulfillment or to draw us away from Him into spiritual emptiness.

Jesus Himself addressed the principle of sowing into the Spirit in Matthew 6:19-21 (NIV), where He says, *"Do not store up for yourselves treasures on earth, where moths and vermin destroy, and where thieves break in and steal. But store up for yourselves treasures in heaven, where moths and vermin do not destroy, and where thieves do not break in and steal. For where your treasure is, there your heart will be also."* The environments we choose—both physically and spiritually—reflect where we are sowing our treasures. If we focus on spiritual growth, the eternal rewards will far outweigh anything the flesh can offer.

Creating environments that foster spiritual growth requires intentionality. It requires making choices about what we expose ourselves to, who we spend time with, and how we engage with God. By cultivating environments that sow into the Spirit, we set the stage for deeper faith, stronger character, and a closer relationship with God.

In conclusion, our spiritual growth is deeply affected by the environments we choose to live in. Surrounding ourselves with a godly community, dedicating personal time to prayer and reflection, avoiding environments that stunt spiritual growth, and making intentional choices to sow into the Spirit are essential steps in nurturing our relationship with God. Remember, the environments we create and engage with either lead us closer to God's purpose or further away. Choose wisely, for the impact on your spiritual journey is profound.

CHAPTER 6: THE ROLE OF VISUALIZATION IN SHAPING ENVIRONMENT

6.1 Vision and Surroundings

Visualization is a powerful tool that bridges the gap between where you are and where you aspire to be. It's the practice of imagining your future success, which can have a profound influence on your present actions and decisions. Your physical environment plays a crucial role in this process, as it serves as a reflection of your vision, goals, and aspirations. By shaping your surroundings to reflect the future you desire, you create an atmosphere that continually motivates and guides you toward achieving those dreams.

Proverbs 29:18 (KJV) says, *"Where there is no vision, the people perish."* Vision is not just about imagining what could be; it's about setting a clear direction for your life. Your environment is one of the ways you can continually reinforce that vision. For example, if your goal is to become healthier, you can set up your home environment in a way that supports that vision—placing fitness equipment in easy-to-access places, stocking your kitchen with healthy foods, and displaying visual reminders of your fitness goals.

Think about how your current environment reflects (or doesn't reflect) your aspirations. Does your living space motivate you to reach for your goals, or does it keep you stagnant? If your goal is to grow spiritually, does your environment encourage you to spend time in prayer and study the Word, or does it distract you with other things? Isaiah 26:3 (NIV) reminds us, *"You will keep in perfect peace those whose minds are steadfast, because they trust in you."* Your environment can help keep your mind steadfast, focused on your vision, and aligned with God's plan for your life.

To reflect your dreams and aspirations in your physical environment, it's important to be intentional about every detail. The way you design and organize your surroundings can act as a constant reminder of your goals and inspire you to stay on track. Whether it's your home, workspace, or any other setting, the environment you create should reflect where you're going, not just where you are.

6.2 Visualization Practices

One of the most effective ways to shape your environment in line with your vision is through visualization practices—tools like vision boards, visual reminders, and daily affirmations that keep your goals at the forefront of your mind. Visualization is not just wishful thinking; it's an intentional practice of seeing yourself in the future and allowing that image to guide your present actions.

Vision boards are one of the most popular visualization tools. They are physical or digital boards where you display images, quotes, and reminders that reflect your dreams and goals. By placing this board in a prominent location, you are constantly reminded of what you are working toward. For example, if you aspire to build a successful business, your vision board might include images of entrepreneurs you admire, quotes about perseverance, and pictures that represent your future business.

Visualization works because the human brain responds to imagery in a powerful way. When you visualize success, you activate the same brain regions that would be engaged if you were actually experiencing that success. This creates a mental pathway that encourages you to take the necessary steps to turn that vision into reality. Habakkuk 2:2 (NIV) states, *"Write down the revelation and make it plain on tablets so that a herald may run with it."* Writing down your vision or creating a visual representation of it helps make the intangible tangible, motivating you to act on it.

Let's consider Axel's story, which exemplifies the power of visualization. Axel dreamed of playing in the NBA or NFL. He was so dedicated to his vision that he transformed his environment to reflect his dreams. He surrounded himself with visual reminders of the athletes he admired—posters on the walls, inspirational quotes, and imagery that symbolized athletic success. Axel's environment became a constant source of motivation, pushing him to train harder, focus more, and align his life with his dreams.

Though Axel may not have made it to the NBA or NFL, his dedication to visualization and aligning his environment with his dreams demonstrates the power of surrounding yourself with the right influences. His commitment to creating an environment that reflected his aspirations helped him stay focused and disciplined, regardless of the outcome.

In addition to vision boards, other visual reminders can be equally effective. These might include placing Scripture verses around your home that reinforce your faith or writing down your goals and keeping them in a visible place. Whether it's a list on your desk, a motivational quote on your wall, or an affirmation on your bathroom mirror, these reminders help anchor your vision in your daily life.

Philippians 4:8 (NIV) encourages us to focus on what is positive and uplifting: *"Finally, brothers and sisters, whatever is true, whatever is noble, whatever is right, whatever is pure, whatever is lovely, whatever is admirable—if anything is excellent or praiseworthy—*

think about such things." Surrounding yourself with visual cues that reflect these values helps you stay focused on what is good and worthy of pursuit.

6.3 The Environment as a Reflection of Your Future Self

Your environment should not only reflect your current goals but also serve as a reminder of the future self you are striving to become. When you design your environment to align with the identity you want to achieve, you are actively shaping the path that will lead you there. Every decision you make about your space should point toward the person you are becoming.

For example, if your goal is to become more disciplined, your environment should reflect habits of discipline. This might mean setting up a workspace that eliminates distractions or organizing your day in a way that prioritizes productivity. If your goal is to deepen your faith, your environment should reflect that aspiration—perhaps by creating a dedicated space for prayer, Bible study, or meditation.

As you design your environment, consider who you want to become in the future. Are there aspects of your environment that are holding you back from stepping into that identity? Are there changes you can make that would encourage growth in that direction? Romans 12:2 (NIV) reminds us, *"Do not conform to the pattern of this world, but be transformed by the renewing of your mind. Then you will be able to test and approve what God's will is—his good, pleasing and perfect will."* Renewing your mind is often about renewing your surroundings to reflect God's will and your own vision for the future.

Think of your environment as a training ground for the person you are becoming. Every time you step into a space that is aligned with your future goals, you are reminded of your purpose and motivated to take action. The more you immerse yourself in an environment that reflects your desired future, the more you will begin to embody that identity.

In practical terms, designing spaces that promote the identity you want to achieve could include small but significant changes. For example, if your goal is to become an author, you might set up a dedicated writing space with books that inspire you, a comfortable desk, and tools that help you focus. If your goal is to grow in leadership, you might display books, quotes, and reminders that reflect leadership values. Everything in your environment should serve as a reflection of the future you are working toward.

Creating this alignment between your environment and your future self requires intentionality. 1 Peter 1:13 (NIV) says, *"Therefore, with minds that are alert and fully sober, set your hope on the grace to be brought to you when Jesus Christ is revealed at his coming."* This verse speaks to the importance of being mentally and spiritually prepared, which also applies to designing an environment that prepares you for the future.

In conclusion, your environment plays a powerful role in shaping not only your present actions but also your future identity. By using tools like vision boards and visual reminders, and by designing spaces that reflect your dreams and goals, you can create an environment that continually pushes you toward success. Remember, your surroundings are not just a reflection of who you are now, but also of who you are

becoming. Shape them wisely, and they will help guide
you to your future self.

CHAPTER 7: THE SCIENTIFIC BASIS FOR ENVIRONMENTAL INFLUENCE

7.1 The Power of Choice Architecture

Choice architecture refers to the design of environments in ways that influence the decisions people make. Small changes in how options are presented or arranged can have a profound impact on behavior without the need for conscious effort. The principle behind choice architecture is simple: when the environment is structured in a way that makes desired behaviors easier or more attractive, people are more likely to follow through with those behaviors.

An example of this can be seen in everyday decisions, such as healthy eating. If you arrange your kitchen so that fruits and vegetables are readily visible and accessible, while junk food is hidden or more difficult to reach, you are likely to make healthier choices without even realizing it. This principle is rooted in the idea that humans tend to choose the path of least resistance. By making positive choices more convenient, the environment subtly nudges people toward better behavior.

In Proverbs 4:26-27 (NIV), we are advised, *"Give careful thought to the paths for your feet and be steadfast in all your ways. Do not turn to the right or the left; keep your foot from evil."* This scripture encourages intentionality in the choices we make, and by extension, in how we structure our environments to facilitate those choices.

One of the most famous examples of choice architecture is seen in the context of food placement in cafeterias. Studies have shown that simply placing healthier food options at eye level and in prominent positions can significantly increase their consumption, while less healthy options that are placed out of immediate sight tend to be chosen less frequently. These small changes in the environment lead to substantial behavioral shifts without requiring people to consciously exert more willpower.

The Bible encourages us to make wise choices and avoid unnecessary temptation. Matthew 26:41 (NIV) says, *"Watch and pray so that you will not fall into temptation. The spirit is willing, but the flesh is weak."* By designing our environment in a way that reduces temptation, we are better equipped to make decisions that align with our values and goals, even when our willpower is low.

7.2 The Role of Cognitive Load

Cognitive load refers to the amount of mental effort required to process information and make decisions. When we are faced with too many choices or too much complexity, our brains become overwhelmed, and decision-making becomes more difficult. This often leads to decision fatigue, where we make poorer choices simply because we are mentally exhausted.

A well-designed environment reduces cognitive load by simplifying choices and removing unnecessary distractions. When your environment is set up in a way that eliminates constant decision-making, you free up mental energy for more important tasks. For instance, setting up your workspace so that all the tools you need are within easy reach reduces the number of decisions you have to make throughout the day, allowing you to focus on your work rather than being distracted by disorganization.

James Clear, author of *Atomic Habits*, emphasizes that reducing cognitive load through environmental design can make positive behaviors more automatic. For example, if you want to read more books, you can reduce cognitive load by keeping books visible and easily accessible in areas where you spend a lot of time. Instead of having to decide whether to read or where to find a book, the environment nudges you toward the desired behavior.

The Bible touches on the importance of focus and mental clarity in several passages. Philippians 4:8 (NIV) says, *"Finally, brothers and sisters, whatever is true, whatever is noble, whatever is right, whatever is pure, whatever is lovely, whatever is admirable—if anything is excellent or praiseworthy—think about such things."* When we reduce the cognitive load in our environment, we create the mental space needed to focus on what is pure, right, and praiseworthy.

By designing your environment to minimize distractions and reduce cognitive load, you can preserve your mental energy for the things that truly matter, enabling you to be more productive and make better decisions.

7.3 Real-World Examples:

Mike's struggle with sweets is a perfect example of how a simple change in the environment can lead to significant behavioral changes. Mike loved sweets, but he also knew that his sugar habit was negatively impacting his health. Despite his best efforts to resist temptation, he often found himself reaching for candy or sugary snacks when they were within easy reach.

Frustrated with his lack of progress, Mike decided to change his environment rather than rely on willpower alone. He made a few key changes to his kitchen. First, he removed all sugary snacks from visible places and stored them in hard-to-reach cabinets. Then, he placed healthier alternatives, such as fruits and nuts, in visible bowls on the kitchen counter. By simply rearranging the physical environment, Mike reduced the temptation to eat sweets and made healthier choices more convenient.

Within a few weeks, Mike noticed a dramatic change in his eating habits. Without having to constantly fight temptation, he found it much easier to stick to his health goals. This simple change in his environment had a profound impact on his behavior, proving that sometimes the key to success lies not in exerting more willpower but in designing an environment that makes the right choices easier.

Mike's story is a powerful illustration of Proverbs 13:20 (NIV), *"Walk with the wise and become wise, for a companion of fools suffers harm."* While this verse speaks to the importance of surrounding ourselves with wise people, the principle applies to all areas of life. When we surround ourselves with environments that promote wisdom and good choices, we are more likely to succeed. Conversely, when we remain in environments that promote temptation or poor decisions, we suffer the consequences.

This principle applies to many areas of life beyond just eating habits. Whether it's organizing your finances, setting up a productive workspace, or creating a routine for spiritual growth, changing small elements of your environment can lead to significant improvements in your behavior and outcomes.

Other real-world examples include the use of checklists to reduce cognitive load and improve consistency in decision-making. Surgeons, pilots, and even successful businesspeople often use checklists to ensure that they make the right decisions every time. This simple environmental tool reduces the mental effort required to remember important steps and helps prevent mistakes, much like the changes Mike made to his kitchen environment.

In conclusion, the scientific basis for environmental influence demonstrates that small changes in our surroundings can lead to significant shifts in behavior. By leveraging the power of choice architecture, reducing cognitive load, and making intentional adjustments to our environment, we can improve our decision-making and achieve our goals more effectively. The stories of individuals like Mike remind us that often, the key to success is not found in exerting more effort but in designing environments that make success easier and more natural.

CHAPTER 8: CHANGING YOUR ENVIRONMENT FOR TRANSFORMATION

8.1 Step-by-Step Guide to Evaluating Your Current Environment

Before transformation can occur, it's important to take stock of your current environment. Many of the habits, behaviors, and outcomes in your life are influenced by the environments you've built around yourself—whether intentionally or unintentionally. Evaluating your physical and social surroundings is the first step in creating meaningful change.

Step 1: Assess Your Physical Space - Begin by evaluating the spaces where you spend the most time—your home, your workspace, and any other environments that are central to your daily life. Ask yourself the following questions:

- Does my physical environment support my goals?
- Is my space organized, or is it cluttered and chaotic?
- Does this environment inspire focus, productivity, and peace, or does it create distractions and stress?
- Are there any elements of my environment that hinder my personal or spiritual growth?

For example, if you are trying to establish a daily prayer routine, is there a quiet, peaceful space in your home where you can pray without distractions? If not, that may be an area where changes are needed. Similarly, if you're aiming to improve your health, is your kitchen organized in a way that encourages healthy eating, or is it filled with temptations that derail your efforts?

The Bible speaks to the importance of order and clarity. In 1 Corinthians 14:40 (NIV), we are instructed, *"But everything should be done in a fitting and orderly way."* Disorder in your physical space can lead to disorder in your mind, making it harder to focus on what truly matters.

Step 2: Evaluate Your Social Environment - Your social circle is just as important as your physical environment. Proverbs 13:20 (NIV) says, *"Walk with the wise and become wise, for a companion of fools suffers harm."* The people you spend time with influence your mindset, behavior, and the choices you make. Consider the following:

- Are the people around you encouraging you to grow, or are they holding you back?
- Are you surrounded by positive influences, or do you spend time with those who engage in negative behaviors or thinking?
- Is your social environment one of mutual support and accountability, or are your relationships more draining than uplifting?

Recognizing the influence of your social circle is key to transforming your environment for growth. Negative relationships or toxic social environments can be just as harmful as a cluttered home or disorganized workspace. Identifying these influences allows you to take proactive steps to either improve those relationships or limit your exposure to them.

Step 3: Reflect on Your Digital Environment - In today's world, your digital environment also plays a huge role in shaping your behavior. This includes the media you consume, the social media platforms you engage with, and the digital tools you use. Ask yourself:

- Is my digital environment aligned with my goals, or is it a source of distraction?
- Do the things I engage with online build me up spiritually, mentally, or emotionally?
- Are there any digital influences—such as certain websites, apps, or contacts—that I need to limit or eliminate?

By reflecting on your physical, social, and digital environments, you can start to see where adjustments are needed. This process of evaluation creates awareness, allowing you to take responsibility for your surroundings and begin making conscious changes.

8.2 Creating a New Environment

Once you've evaluated your current environment, the next step is to create a new one that is more conducive to your growth. This is not a process that happens overnight. Transformation is often gradual, but with intentional steps, you can shift your environment to one that aligns with your goals and values.

Step 1: Start with Small Changes - The easiest way to begin transforming your environment is by making small, manageable changes. Start with one area of your life—perhaps your workspace or your morning routine—and identify one or two small adjustments you can make. For example, if your goal is to spend more time in Bible study, you might designate a specific chair or desk as your study space and leave your Bible and journal there, ready to go. These small changes help you develop new habits that will gradually lead to bigger transformations.

In Zechariah 4:10 (NLT), we are reminded, *"Do not despise these small beginnings, for the Lord rejoices to see the work begin."* Even the smallest changes can lead to significant results when they are made intentionally.

Step 2: Remove Obstacles and Add Positive Triggers - Identify anything in your environment that might be hindering your progress and gradually begin to remove those obstacles. This could mean decluttering a space, limiting time with certain negative influences, or reducing distractions in your daily routine. At the same time, add positive triggers that will encourage growth. These could be reminders of your goals, inspirational quotes, or new habits that align with your vision.

If, for example, you are trying to eat healthier, you can remove junk food from your kitchen and replace it with nutritious snacks. Or if you want to strengthen your prayer life, you can set up a quiet space in your home and keep it stocked with your Bible, devotionals, and a comfortable chair.

Step 3: Gradually Expand the Change - As you begin to experience the benefits of these small adjustments, you can expand the transformation to other areas of your environment. If you started with your home, you might now focus on your workspace. If you began by shifting your physical environment, you might now examine your social circle. The goal is to create consistency across all areas of your life so that every environment you engage with supports your growth and well-being.

Psalm 37:23 (NIV) says, *"The Lord makes firm the steps of the one who delights in him."* As you gradually shift into new environments, trust that God is guiding your steps. With each adjustment, you are building a more supportive space that will help you reach your goals.

8.3 The Digital Diet

As you create a new environment to foster your growth, it's important not to overlook one of the most pervasive aspects of modern life—your digital environment. In today's world, what we consume digitally is as influential as the people we surround ourselves with. In today's world, our environment isn't limited to physical spaces and people—it includes our digital environment. We must be as intentional about what we consume digitally as we are about the physical food we eat. This is where the concept of a "Digital Diet" comes into play.

Just as we manage our diets carefully—choosing what to eat and drink to nourish our bodies—we must be conscious of what we watch, read, hear, and listen to, in order to protect our minds and spirits. What we feed into our minds can either nurture or hinder our personal growth. Philippians 4:8 (NIV) guides us to *"think about such things"* that are true, noble, right, pure, lovely, admirable, excellent, and praiseworthy.

Being mindful of your digital diet means limiting exposure to negative, unproductive, or damaging content. Consider what you regularly consume:

- What are you watching on television or social media?
- What are you reading?
- What music, podcasts, or other audio do you regularly listen to?

Just as an unhealthy physical diet can lead to sickness, an unhealthy digital diet can affect your mental and spiritual well-being. Be careful to feed your eyes and mind with content that aligns with the person you want to become. Intentional choices in your digital consumption will influence your mindset, attitude, and ultimately your success.

8.4 Long-Term Sustainability

Creating a new environment is only the beginning. To experience lasting transformation, it's essential to maintain and adapt your environment as you continue to grow. What works for you today might not be as effective in the future, so it's important to regularly assess and refine your environment to match your evolving goals and needs.

Step 1: Regularly Evaluate Your Progress - Make it a habit to periodically evaluate your environment to ensure that it is still serving your growth. You might schedule regular check-ins with yourself—monthly or quarterly—to reflect on how your surroundings are impacting your progress. Are there areas where you've fallen back into old habits? Are there new goals that require further changes? Proverbs 4:23 (NIV) advises, *"Above all else, guard your heart, for everything you do flows from it."* Regular reflection allows you to guard your heart and mind by continually aligning your environment with your purpose.

Step 2: Be Willing to Make Adjustments - As you grow and evolve, your needs will change, and your environment should change with you. What served you in one season of life may no longer be effective in another. Don't be afraid to make adjustments when necessary. This might mean rearranging your workspace, reevaluating your social circle, or setting new digital boundaries.

In Isaiah 43:19 (NIV), God says, *"See, I am doing a new thing! Now it springs up; do you not perceive it?"* As God does new things in your life, be open to adapting your environment to support the new directions He is leading you in.

Step 3: Build Systems for Consistency - One of the keys to long-term sustainability is building systems that help maintain the positive changes you've made. For example, you might establish a cleaning routine to keep your home or workspace organized. You might set boundaries with your time or social media use to avoid falling back into old habits. By creating systems that support your environment, you make it easier to maintain the changes you've worked so hard to implement.

Matthew 7:24-25 (NIV) speaks of building on a solid foundation: *"Therefore everyone who hears these words of mine and puts them into practice is like a wise man who built his house on the rock. The rain came down, the streams rose, and the winds blew and beat against that house; yet it did not fall, because it had its foundation on the rock."* A well-structured environment acts as a strong foundation that can withstand life's challenges, helping you stay grounded even in difficult times.

In conclusion, transforming your environment is a powerful way to support your personal and spiritual growth. By evaluating your current surroundings, making gradual changes, and maintaining those changes over time, you create a space that aligns with your vision and goals. Remember that transformation is a journey, not a destination. As you continue to grow, be open to adapting your environment to support each new season of life.

CHAPTER 9: ENVIRONMENT AND PERSONAL IDENTITY

9.1 You Are a Product of Your Environment

The environments we grow up in significantly shape who we become—our mindset, our outlook on life, and even our understanding of ourselves. From an early age, the home, community, and cultural surroundings we are exposed to play a critical role in forming our personal identity. These environments influence our beliefs about what is possible, what is normal, and what we are capable of achieving.

Consider the profound impact that being raised in a positive, supportive environment has on a person. If someone grows up surrounded by love, encouragement, and opportunities, they are more likely to develop a confident, growth-oriented mindset. They are taught, often unconsciously, that the world is a place full of possibilities. In contrast, individuals who grow up in environments of negativity, fear, or scarcity may develop limiting beliefs, such as feeling unworthy or incapable of success.

The Bible illustrates the importance of a supportive environment in shaping our identity. Proverbs 22:6 (NIV) says, *"Start children off on the way they should go, and even when they are old they will not turn from it."* This verse highlights how foundational the early environment is in shaping one's direction in life. The lessons and behaviors instilled in childhood often carry through to adulthood, influencing how people perceive themselves and the world around them.

Our identity is shaped not only by our upbringing but also by the societal expectations and norms of the environment we live in. Communities, schools, and even media can either reinforce our potential or impose limitations on what we believe we can achieve. Over time, these influences become ingrained in our thinking, forming the core of who we believe we are.

Just as a seed's potential is determined by the quality of the soil it is planted in, so too does the environment determine how much of our potential we can truly realize. Even the best seed will struggle to thrive if planted in poor soil. Similarly, no matter how strong or capable a person is, their environment sets limits on how far they can grow.

Consider the example of a shark. When placed in an aquarium, a shark's growth is restricted to just a few inches, regardless of how long it remains there. However, when released into the vast ocean, that same shark can grow to its full potential. The limitation was never in the shark—it was in the environment.

In the same way, humans often find that certain environments stifle their growth. These environments, like the aquarium for the shark, prevent them from reaching their full potential. To flourish, you must be intentional about choosing an environment that nurtures your development, much like selecting rich soil for a seed. The more you nurture your environment, the better the results you will see in your personal growth.

Creating an Environment That Fosters Growth

If you find yourself in an environment that limits your potential, the first step is recognizing the need for change. Just as a seed can be replanted in fertile soil, you have the ability to shift your surroundings to better support your growth. Here's how:

1. **Evaluate Your Current Environment:** Start by assessing whether your current environment—physical, social, and mental—is conducive to your growth. Are you surrounded by negativity, distractions, or limitations that are keeping you from flourishing? Recognizing these constraints is the first step to transformation.

2. **Seek Out New Opportunities:** If you are in a restrictive environment, look for ways to broaden your horizons. This could mean seeking new professional opportunities, connecting with growth-oriented individuals, or finding communities that challenge you to be your best. Philippians 3:13-14 (NIV) says, *"Forgetting what is behind and straining toward what is ahead, I press on toward the goal to win the prize for*

which God has called me heavenward in Christ Jesus." Pressing on often means leaving behind environments that no longer serve you.

3. **Create a Nurturing Space:** You don't always have to move to an entirely new environment. Sometimes, you can transform your current surroundings by making small but impactful changes. Remove distractions and toxic influences, and fill your space with reminders of your goals, values, and faith. Surround yourself with people who lift you up and help you reach your potential. Proverbs 27:17 (NIV) says, *"As iron sharpens iron, so one person sharpens another."* Building relationships with others who foster growth is essential.

4. **Reprogram Your Mindset:** Even if you can't immediately change your physical environment, you can begin by changing your mental environment. Reprogram limiting beliefs and adopt a growth mindset. Meditate on Scripture, focus on positive affirmations, and fill your mind with things that align with the person you want to become. Romans 12:2 (NIV) says, *"Do not*

conform to the pattern of this world, but be transformed by the renewing of your mind." Your environment is not just external; it starts within your mind.

In the same way that a shark needs the ocean to grow to its full size, you need an environment that provides the space, nutrients, and support necessary for you to reach your potential. Be intentional about cultivating environments—both external and internal—that align with your highest aspirations and goals.

9.2 Breaking Free from Negative Conditioning

For those who grew up in toxic or limiting environments, breaking free from the negative conditioning that was imposed on them can be challenging. These environments may have instilled feelings of unworthiness, fear, or insecurity, all of which can limit personal growth and prevent individuals from living out their full potential. The good news is that, through intentional effort, it is possible to overcome these limiting beliefs and break free from the chains of a toxic environment.

One of the first steps toward breaking free is recognizing the negative conditioning you've absorbed. Romans 12:2 (NIV) offers a powerful call to renewal: *"Do not conform to the pattern of this world, but be transformed by the renewing of your mind. Then you will be able to test and approve what God's will is— his good, pleasing and perfect will."* The transformation begins with renewing the mind—challenging the limiting beliefs that have been imposed by the toxic environment and replacing them with the truth of who God says you are.

Here are several strategies to break free from negative conditioning:

1. **Identify and Challenge Limiting Beliefs**: Start by identifying the specific beliefs you've internalized that hold you back. Are there messages from your childhood or past experiences that lead you to believe you aren't capable of success? Once you've identified these beliefs, challenge their validity. Are they truly grounded in reality, or are they the result of someone else's fears or insecurities projected onto you?

2. **Surround Yourself with Positive Influences**: Just as a toxic environment can damage your mindset, a positive, growth-oriented environment can uplift and transform you. Seek out relationships and communities that reinforce your worth, potential, and growth. Proverbs 27:17 (NIV) says, *"As iron sharpens iron, so one person sharpens another."* Surrounding yourself with individuals who encourage and support you is key to breaking free from the limitations of a toxic past.

3. **Use Affirmations and Scripture**: Reprogramming your mind with positive affirmations and the truth of Scripture can help counteract the negative conditioning of your past. For example, if you struggle with feelings of unworthiness, remind yourself of 1 Peter 2:9 (NIV), which says, *"But you are a chosen people, a royal priesthood, a holy nation, God's special possession, that you may declare the praises of him who called you out of darkness into his wonderful light."* By meditating on such verses,

you are replacing the lies of a toxic environment with the truth of your identity in Christ.

4. **Develop a Growth Mindset**: A fixed mindset keeps you stuck in the belief that your abilities are limited and cannot be changed, while a growth mindset sees challenges as opportunities for development. By adopting a growth mindset, you empower yourself to see beyond the limitations imposed by your past environment. You begin to understand that with effort and perseverance, you can break free and achieve your full potential.

Breaking free from negative conditioning takes time, but with persistence and faith, you can transform your thinking and step into a new reality.

9.3 The Power of Reprogramming

Once you've identified and begun to break free from negative conditioning, the next step is to actively choose new environments that align with your desired identity and values. This process of reprogramming is about intentionally creating a space—physically, socially, and mentally—that reinforces the person you want to become, rather than who you were told you were.

Your environment should be a reflection of your highest aspirations, supporting the identity you are working to cultivate. Galatians 6:7-8 (NIV) provides a foundational principle for this: *"Do not be deceived: God cannot be mocked. A man reaps what he sows. Whoever sows to please their flesh, from the flesh will reap destruction; whoever sows to please the Spirit, from the Spirit will reap eternal life."* By choosing environments that nurture your spiritual and personal growth, you are sowing seeds that will yield a harvest of positive change in your life.

Here are some ways to reprogram your environment:

1. **Physically Reorganize Your Space**: Just as you clear out mental clutter, it's important to clear out physical clutter as well. Reorganize your living and workspaces to reflect your new identity. Remove anything that reminds you of negative past experiences or unhealthy habits and replace them with items that inspire and

motivate you toward your goals. This might include creating a dedicated space for prayer or reflection, placing visual reminders of your aspirations in your home, or redesigning your workspace to promote productivity and focus.

2. **Seek Out New Social Circles**: As you grow and change, it may be necessary to distance yourself from relationships that no longer serve your new identity. This doesn't mean abandoning people who care about you, but it may mean setting boundaries with individuals who try to pull you back into old patterns. Instead, seek out social circles and communities that align with your values and goals. Hebrews 10:24-25 (NIV) says, *"And let us consider how we may spur one another on toward love and good deeds, not giving up meeting together, as some are in the habit of doing, but encouraging one another—and all the more as you see the Day approaching."* Building relationships with people who encourage your growth is crucial to maintaining your progress.

3. **Feed Your Mind with Positive Inputs**: The media you consume plays a major role in shaping your thoughts and beliefs. Choose books, podcasts, sermons, and other media that reinforce your values and your desired identity. Philippians 4:8 (NIV) offers wise guidance: *"Finally, brothers and sisters, whatever is true, whatever is noble, whatever is right, whatever is pure, whatever is lovely, whatever is admirable—if anything is excellent or praiseworthy—think about such things."* By feeding your mind with positive, uplifting content, you reprogram your mindset to align with your future self.

4. **Embrace New Habits and Routines**: Your daily habits are a reflection of your identity. By changing your habits, you can reinforce the new identity you are stepping into. For example, if your goal is to become more disciplined, start by creating a morning routine that sets the tone for your day. If you want to grow spiritually, commit to daily prayer or Bible study. These small, consistent habits have a cumulative effect and help solidify the transformation in your life.

As you continue to reprogram your environment, you'll find that your surroundings begin to work in your favor rather than against you. Over time, these intentional changes will lead to lasting transformation, helping you align more closely with your desired identity and values.

Just as a shark in a fish tank will only grow to 8 inches but can grow over 8 feet in the ocean, humans are similarly limited by the environments they inhabit. The shark will never outgrow its environment, and neither will we. Often, we find ourselves surrounded by small-minded, limiting influences that stifle our growth. But just as a shark's potential is fully realized in the ocean, you, too, must seek out an expansive, growth-oriented environment to unlock your potential.

"We become part of what we are around." This principle rings true in all aspects of life. If you surround yourself with small-thinking people, you limit your ability to think big, dream boldly, and grow. As Jim Rohn wisely observed, *"Successful people have libraries. The rest have big-screen TVs."* The people, things, and ideas we surround ourselves with are either tools for growth or distractions that lead to stagnation.

Shane Parrish reminds us: "Distance yourself from the people that you don't want to become." This underscores the importance of intentionally choosing relationships that align with your goals and values. By surrounding yourself with people who encourage and challenge you, you create an environment that promotes personal and spiritual growth. Distance yourself from those who limit your potential and watch as your personal development accelerates.

In conclusion, your environment plays a crucial role in shaping your personal identity. Whether you are influenced by your upbringing or the societal norms around you, you have the power to break free from negative conditioning and reprogram your surroundings to reflect who you truly want to become. By choosing new environments that align with your values and goals, you set yourself on a path toward personal and spiritual growth, allowing you to live in alignment with your highest aspirations.

CONCLUSION: THE ENVIRONMENT-BEHAVIOR CONNECTION

Summarizing the Core Insights

Throughout this book, we have explored the profound connection between the environment and behavior. Your surroundings—whether physical, social, or mental—play a vital role in shaping who you are, what you believe, and how you act. From the design of your home and workspace to the people you associate with, every aspect of your environment influences the choices you make and the person you become.

We have seen how:

- **Physical spaces** can inspire productivity, focus, and peace or lead to distraction, stress, and stagnation. The arrangement of your surroundings has the power to either support or hinder your growth.

- **Social environments** can uplift and encourage you to pursue your goals or weigh you down with negativity, doubt, and unhealthy habits. The people you spend time with shape your mindset and can either propel you forward or hold you back.

- **Mental and digital environments** also shape your thinking. The content you consume, the habits you cultivate, and the routines you follow determine your mindset and ultimately your outcomes.

As Proverbs 4:23 (NIV) wisely counsels, *"Above all else, guard your heart, for everything you do flows from it."* Your environment is directly connected to the condition of your heart and mind, and it influences every decision you make.

Understanding the environment-behavior connection empowers you to take control of your surroundings. You are not merely a passive participant in life, shaped by external factors beyond your control; rather, you have the power to actively design your environment to align with your goals and values. By doing so, you create conditions where growth, success, and spiritual development are not only possible but inevitable.

The Power of Awareness

Awareness is the key to unlocking the power of your environment. As we've discussed, many of the influences around us are subtle—often acting in ways we don't immediately notice. But by becoming conscious of your environment and its impact on your behavior, you take the first step toward creating positive change.

Assessing your environment regularly allows you to identify areas that need improvement and make necessary adjustments. This process is ongoing; as you grow and evolve, your environment should evolve with you. What worked for you in the past may no longer serve you in the future, and being aware of these changes enables you to continuously refine your surroundings for optimal growth.

James 1:5 (NIV) reminds us, *"If any of you lacks wisdom, you should ask God, who gives generously to all without finding fault, and it will be given to you."* Wisdom allows us to evaluate our environment with discernment and make informed decisions about the changes we need to make. With God's guidance, we can learn to recognize both the positive and negative influences in our surroundings and respond accordingly.

Regular self-reflection is an essential part of this process. Take time to ask yourself:

- Is my current environment helping or hindering my personal and spiritual growth?
- Are there elements of my environment—physical, social, or digital—that no longer serve my goals?
- What small changes can I make to create a more supportive and empowering environment?

By remaining vigilant and continuously assessing your environment, you ensure that it remains aligned with your vision for the future. This level of awareness will help you stay focused on your goals and open the door to ongoing transformation.

Take Control of Your Environment to Unlock Your Full Potential

The message of this book is simple but powerful: your environment shapes your life. But you are not powerless in the face of these influences. You have the ability—and the responsibility—to take control of your surroundings and design an environment that supports your highest potential.

As we have discussed throughout these chapters, small changes in your environment can lead to significant shifts in behavior. Whether it's decluttering your home, surrounding yourself with positive influences, or establishing daily routines that align with your goals, each intentional decision brings you one step closer to living the life you desire.

Colossians 3:23-24 (NIV) reminds us, *"Whatever you do, work at it with all your heart, as working for the Lord, not for human masters, since you know that you will receive an inheritance from the Lord as a reward."* This scripture calls us to approach every area of life with intentionality and purpose. Taking control of your environment is part of this process—it is an act of stewardship over the life God has given you.

As you move forward, let this be your call to action:

- **Evaluate your environment regularly.** Identify the physical, social, and digital influences that are shaping your life, and make changes where necessary.

- **Design your surroundings with intention.** Align your environment with your goals, dreams, and values, creating a space that fosters growth and supports your highest aspirations.

- **Take small steps consistently.** Transformation doesn't happen overnight, but each small change adds up over time. Stay committed to the process, and trust that your efforts will yield fruit.

Remember, the power to change your environment lies in your hands. By taking control of your surroundings, you can unlock your full potential and live a life that reflects your true identity and purpose.

With this final chapter, we bring together the key insights from this book. Your environment is a powerful force in shaping your behavior, but through awareness, intentional design, and consistent action, you can harness that power to create the life you want to live. Take control of your environment and watch as it transforms not only your behavior but also your mindset, your spirit, and your future.

ABOUT THE AUTHOR

Nick Imoru is a dynamic speaker, author, educator, entrepreneur, and consultant based in Canada. He is the President of Achievers Centre, a division of Philips Reliability Consult Inc. Nick's mission is centered on empowering the human spirit through consulting, coaching, connecting and circulating ideas and information. His goal is to inspire, ignite passion, create profit, and make a spiritual impact, ultimately helping individuals bridge the gap between where they are and where they aspire to be.

Nick holds a B.Eng. in Mechanical and Production Engineering and an MSc. in Advanced Technology from the UK. With over 18 years of experience in the Oil and Gas industry, he specializes in Maintenance & Reliability Engineering and is a Certified Maintenance & Reliability Professional (CMRP), reflecting his commitment to excellence in his field.

As the author of over 20 books and numerous articles and research papers, Nick's work spans personal development, spirituality, academia, business, and finance. He is the founder of Achievers Consult, Achievers Centre, and Achievers Publishing, all operating under Philips Reliability Consult Inc.

Nick is happily married to Dr. Margaret and is a proud father of two daughters, Nelly and Myra. His unwavering dedication to personal and professional growth, combined with his entrepreneurial spirit, continues to make a profound impact on individuals and organizations, guiding them towards success and fulfillment.

With a vision to inspire, train, develop, and unlock potential, Nick Imoru is committed to helping individuals and businesses achieve their highest levels of success.

To contact Nick or learn more about Achievers Centre, opportunities, speeches, and seminars, please use the information below:

Email: Nick@achieverscentre.com
Website: www.achieverscentre.com

BOOKS BY SAME AUTHOR

- A Heart for God
- Operating God's Private Lines
- Growing In Life
- Money & Pleasure: Trap of Purpose
- Success Buttons for Life & Academic Excellence
- The Making of Greatness
- Your Best Year Ever
- Nothing Just Happens
- How Did I Become Like This
- Achievers Daily Tonic
- Living in His Fullness: Unveiling the Life, Mission, Death and Triumph of Jesus
- Your Belief System: How Your Thoughts Dictate Your Life
- The Wit & Wisdom of Dr David Oyedepo
- The Tongue: How Your Words Shape Your Destiny

- He Has Said...So We May Boldly Say
- Kings Don't Beg, They Make Decrees
- Character: The Blueprint for a Great Future
- Living in His Light: Understanding Your New Identity in Christ
- Personal & Family Budgeting: Mastering Your Money for Financial Freedom
- Your Money, Your Future: A Student's Guide to Financial Success
- Choosing the Right Path: A Career Guide for Teens and Youth
- The 21 Life Rules Every Child Should Live By
- Saving Your Future: A Practical Guide to Financial Literacy
- Think It, Do It: How to Turn Thoughts into Meaningful Action
- Adventures in God's Amazing Storybook, Part 1
- Adventures in God's Amazing Storybook, Part 2

To order any of these books, please visit:

Our online shop @ www.achieverscentre.com

or any of the amazon websites:

www.amazon.ca or www.amazon.com or www.amazon.co.uk, etc